The Bug House Family Restaurant

Published by Tradewind Books in 2013.
Published in the UK and the US in 2014. Text copyright ©
2013 Beverley Brenna. Illustrations copyright © 2013 Marc Mongeau.
All rights reserved. No part of this publication may be reproduced, stored
in a retrieval system or transmitted, in any form or by any means, with-
out the prior written permission of the publisher or, in the case of pho-
tocopying or other reprographic copying, a license from Access Copyright,
Toronto, Ontario. The right of Beverley Brenna and Marc Mongeau to be
identified as the author and the illustrator of this work has been asserted
by them in accordance with the Copyright, Design and Patents Act 1988.

Book design by Elisa Gutiérrez

Printed in Canada in October 2013 by Sunrise Printing, Vancouver, BC.

LIBRARY AND ARCHIVES CANADA CATALOGUING IN PUBLICATION

Brenna, Beverley A., author
    The bug house family restaurant / by Beverley Brenna ; illustrated
by Marc Mongeau.

ISBN 978-1-926890-01-2 (pbk.)

    I. Mongeau, Marc, illustrator II. Title.

PS8553.R382B85 2013   jC811'.54   C2013-903367-X

. . . .

The publisher thanks the Government of Canada and Canadian Heritage
for their financial support through the Canada Council for the Arts, the
Canada Book Fund and Livres Canada Books. The publisher also thanks
the Government of the Province of British Columbia for the financial support
it has given through the Book Publishing Tax Credit program and the
British Columbia Arts Council.

The Bug House Family Restaurant

by

Beverley Brenna

illustrations by

Marc Mongeau

Tradewind Books

VANCOUVER • LONDON

for Jasper and Sebastian
&
Andrew and Nicholas
with ant hills of love—BB

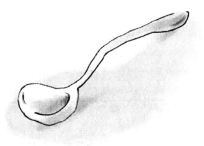

to all the misunderstood insects in the
world—especially the crispy—MM

Contents

Author's Note

It is possible that our food habits may change over the course of the 21st Century. Things at which we used to wrinkle our noses at could become a staple in our diet. Some people already delight in mealworms fried in garlic butter. Recently students from McGill University won The Hult Prize for their idea to cultivate crickets as a food source. Maybe it's just a matter of time . . .

The Bughouse Family Restaurant was conceived as an eatery-waiting-to-happen. The first poem was written in 1986 after a parent sent chocolate covered ants to school and many of my grade 6 students bravely sampled them. I began to write more and more poems while insect recipes beat their tiny wings against my brain. Twenty of the poems won the children's literature category of the 1996 Saskatchewan's Writers' Guild Contest. Encouraged, I wrote three more, and then four, until finally this collection was completed . . . I mean, hatched.

An adult, sickened by some of the poems, once asked me, "Why would you want to think of eating bugs?" and then a kid replied "Why not?" So—why not indeed! Put on your napkins for the poems ahead—some of them are, I admit, a bit wingy.

B.B.

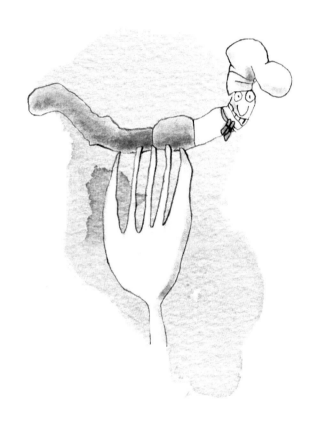

Foreword

Instead of thinking bugs are gross
Please don't be too suspicious.
With half a chance, and one good chef
They could be quite delicious!

Take some **heat**,

CROSS

THE STREET,

Listen to what we **say**

If it **flies**,

If it **CRAWLS**,

Then we've got it

HEY!

Bug House Commercial

If you think you're goin' buggy eatin' burgers and fries . . .
Same old ice cream, same old pies . . .

If you think you're goin' buggy, go all the way
To *The Bug House Restaurant*, come today!

We'll seat you and we'll treat you to wild cuisine!
We've the best bug platters you've ever seen!

Take some heat, cross the street,
Just come over our way . . . If it flies, if it crawls,
Then we've got it
HEY!

If you crave a beetle, an ant or a fly,
The Bug House is the place that'll satisfy.

Daily Specials

On Monday night, *The Bug House* makes
Hundreds of mosquito steaks!
Each mosquito's sliced and fried
And served with spiders on the side.

On Tuesday, count on termite pie
Guaranteed to satisfy.
For the smaller appetite,
Crispy wings are nice and light.

On Wednesday it's hornet soup
By the spoon or by the scoop.
Guaranteed to make you grin,
Order stinger out,
Or in.

On Thursday we have Bug Surprise
Made with centipedes and flies,
Bugs with Cream or A La Mode
And Buggy Breath Mints for the road.

Cooked and served beside your chair,
Fireflies are Friday's fare.
For this very special treat,
Phone ahead to save a seat.

On Saturday we lift the rugs
And boil up the carpet bugs.
Served with leggy Spider Wine—
A perfect way for two to dine.

Sunday night's Aerobic Night
When you must catch your food in flight.
Put your muscles to the test,
It's active dining at its best.

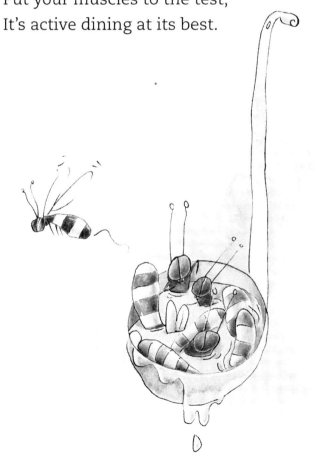

The Gift

I gave candies from *The Bug House*
for Mother's Day this year.
I put them in a pretty box
and printed, "For you, Dear."
So delighted with them,
she did a little dance.
I wonder, should I tell her
they are chocolate covered ANTS?

Uncle Partridge's Collection

Uncle Partridge came to town
Riding in a Chevy,
Left his suitcase in the trunk
Because it was too heavy.

Once when he was busy,
I sneaked outside to see, but
Never saw what was inside
Because I had no key.

Sunday night, he talked to Mom,
And showed a whopping cheque.
"I told them what I had and then,
They paid me all on spec!"

He said it like a secret.
He said it almost weeping.
I knew I had to pick the lock
That night when he was sleeping.

Using just a piece of wire,
A bandaid, and some gum,
I opened up that suitcase and
I saw what he had done.

He'd packed up moths and butterflies,
A million, maybe two,
And now he planned to sell them.
"But where?" I thought. "To who . . ."

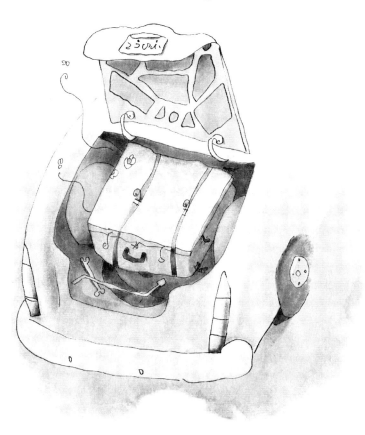

WANT ADS

COOK: Apply at *The Bug House*.

QUALIFICATIONS:

- Must have demonstrated ability to identify bugs.
- Degree in entomology an asset.
- Training with master chef provided.
- Anyone afraid of bats and snakes need not apply.

LIVE BUGS:

Need bugs bagged according to type.

5 cents each for mosquitoes, 10 cents each for anything larger.

Bring them to the back door of *The Bug House* before sunrise.

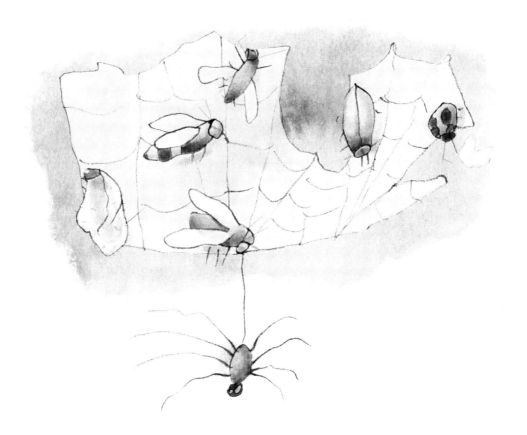

Provincial Ingredients

From B.C. we get beetles;
Alberta sends us ants;
New Brunswick's nine-spot ladybugs
arrive attached to plants.

Nut weevils from Newfoundland
And Nova Scotian gnats
Are sure to please our customers
Especially if they're bats!

Manitoban mites
Add maple to our sauces;
Potato bugs from PEI
Make tantalizing squashes.

Queen bees from Quebec
Are served up à la carte.
Ontarian oyster shells
Give soups and stews their heart.

Labradorian lightning bugs
Are very nice in ices.
And all our buggy provinces
Contribute six-legged spices.

CHORUS:
But . . . spiders are a Saskatchewan snack,
A Saskatchewan snack,
A Saskatchewan snack!
Spiders are a Saskatchewan snack,
And we eat them a leg at a time!

Territorial Specialties

Black Fly Bread:
NWT

Yukon:
Aphid Sprite

Nunavut:
the Iggutaq
or Bumblebee
Delight.

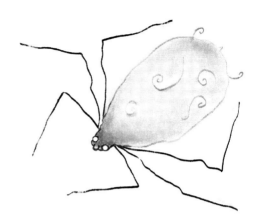

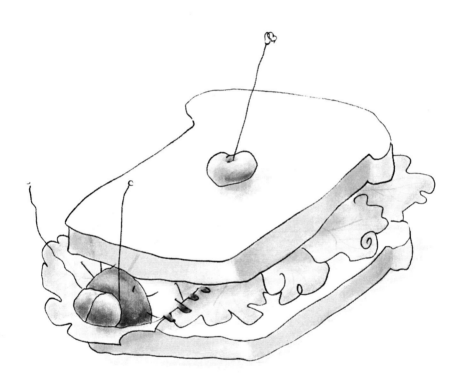

School Lunch

Monday's lunch fell in the river.
I called *The Bug House* to deliver.
To my school they quickly brought
One fresh sandwich, nice and hot!
When I peeked to see the filler,
It was one big caterpillar.

"Someone has to trade with me,"
Whimpered Suzanne Ellis.
"All I have is tunafish
Mixed with sweet green relish!"
I nodded as I offered mine,
And smiled with bravado.
When she asked what kind it was
I told her, "Avocado."

A Picky Eater

"Would you like an ant for tea?"
"I wouldn't," answered Suki Lee.

"Would you like an ant for brunch?"
"I wouldn't," said the girl, "Nor lunch."

"What if they had washed its hair,
Soaped and powdered, taken care
To oil each feeler, salt each toe?"

Certain, Suki answered, "No!"

Kate Eats Bugs

Kate eats bugs.
She told us so.
She said,
There's something
You should know . . .
I like them whole
I like them sliced
I like them plain
I like them spiced.
I can't seem to get enough.
'Cause catching bugs is really tough!

"Here's a bee!" said Abejundio.
"Nope," said Kate. "Too striped."

"What about this gnat?" said Pat.
"Nope," said Kate. "Too hyped."

"Try this ant!" said Dante Hall.
"Nope, won't do," said Kate. "Too small."

"Here's a chrysalis," said Ned. "Just pull!"
"Oh, too bad," said Kate. "I'm full!"

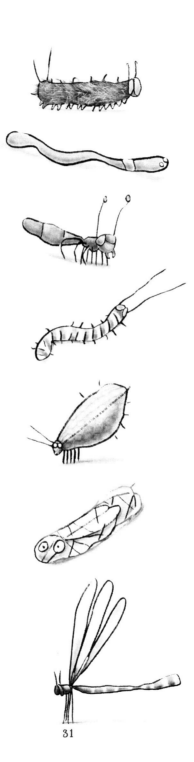

Centipede-Ade

Max the blender
Adds a
Slender
Sprig of mint,
A squeeze of lime,
Dash of parsley,
Pinch of thyme,
Grinds it up with cherry cola
Chills until it's
Cold and colda'
Waits until an order's placed
Then adds the centipedes
To taste . . .

Hervis and Eddy

Hervis and Eddy were terrible twins;
They dined every night on tarantula skins.
Their manners were bad, their language was rude,
And they burped, and they coughed,
                    and they sneezed on their food.

One night they arrived and were led to their chairs—
The object of everyone's whispers and stares,
For Hervis was wearing pajamas and slippers
And Eddy was sporting a snorkel and flippers!

Eager to order, they whistled and howled.
Looking about, they sniffled and scowled.
The waiter went by with melifluous wrath
And Hervis and Eddy leaned into his path.

Then sputtering spittering Eddy jumped up.
He shook and he spat and then drank from his cup
And out of his snorkel with charming aplomb
A bumble of bees darted out . . . minus one . . .

For a moment both Hervis and Eddy were quiet
Then Hervis cried out, "We're both on a diet!"
They hustled along saying, "Thanks," and "Good night,"
Then opened the door and were soon out of sight.

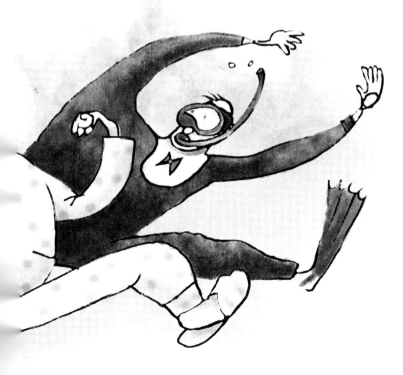

Ants in his Pants

Juan Henry did a little dance.
"Help me, HEY! I've got ants in my pants!
Ants in my pants that are making me WHOOP!
Nippering, zippering, out of my soup."

"Here, there and
Everywhere! That's not fair!
I've even got ants in my UNDERWEAR!"

Bug Sushi

Zoe orders honey bee
But quickly finds it on her knee.

Next she orders butterfly
And sadly sees it flutter by.

When she tries the ladybug
It bounces down on to the rug.

"Waiter, let me pay my bill
I'm feeling worn, I'm feeling ill . . .

Nothing here is . . . well . . . well done . . .
In Motion eating's just no fun!"

When Michael Eats Ladybug Soup

Coming closer—
  An orange full moon—
  Ladybug soup
  On the end of a spoon.

Thick and sticky
It makes him shout
"Open the sky,
  I want to get out!"

Slick and oozy
Above his chin.
He shuts his eyes.
The spoon goes in!

Spoon in his mouth,
Smile in his throat,
A few minutes later
He calls to the waiter.

"Thanks for the soup,
Now double the size;
I'd like another,
And this time with flies!"

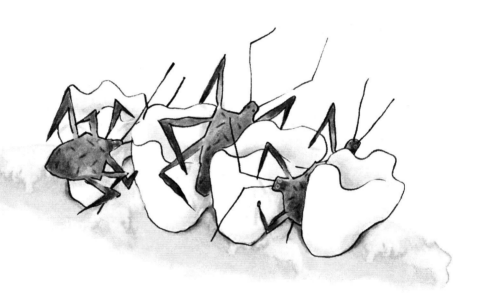

Tooth Bugs

When Johnny opened up his mouth
Stretching wide from north to south

Dr. White said, "Have you brushed?
Have you rinsed and flossed and flushed?"

Johnny answered, "Yes I have . . . "
And then the dentist saw a cav-

ity and other stranger things.
Feelers, wiggling legs, and wings.

The dentist stared from east to west
Until, at last, the boy confessed.

"We do eat out, a lot," he said.
"And sometimes things are not . . . quite . . . dead . . ."

Marly Brown's Birthday

Marly yelled and screamed and kicked,
Marly bit and bawled.
"What in heaven's name is wrong?"
Her worried mother called.

"My party is this afternoon,"
Marly spit and swore.
"All my friends are coming,
And the games will be a bore."

Marly stamped her heavy foot.
She scowled her biggest scowl.
Then Marly opened up her mouth
And howled her loudest howl.

"Hey Marly," said her brother.
"There's something you should know.
The Bug House has a party room
Where all of you could go."

"I want a *Bug House* party!"
Marly shrieked and pulled her hair.
Her mother phoned *The Bug House*
And they had the party there.

The spider in her cider
Made poor Marly scream and shake.
She caterwauled to Winnipeg
Before they served the cake!

Just Dessert

Emmaline Adeline Constantine Bligh
Came through the door with her head held high;
She minced and she winced and she said with a sigh:
"Of course I can't eat . . . well, maybe some pie."

Emmaline Adeline Constantine sat
And gingerly took off her gloves and her hat,
And they rolled in a pie cart longer than t h a t . . .
And she chose, very loudly, "A piece of the gnat!"

Emmaline Adeline took off her shoes
And wiggled her toes while attempting to choose
Again from the trolley—"I just can't refuse
Your butterfly pie—just the greens! Not the blues!"

Emmaline wiped a wing from her knee,
Took off her glasses and waved them for "Three
Of those pastry things there—the wasp and the bee
And that pink one on top—the flan of the flea."

She ate and she sat and she sat and she ate
Until suddenly worried the hour was late,
She licked up the last of the crumbs from her plate,
Wiggled her FEELERS, and said, "That was great!"

Chocolate Covered Bees

What in the world
could be sweeter than these
chocolate covered
honey bees?

With a **squish** and a
     z—i—n—g and a
crunch of a wing they go *down*
                            with a whirr
                            and a tickle of fur.

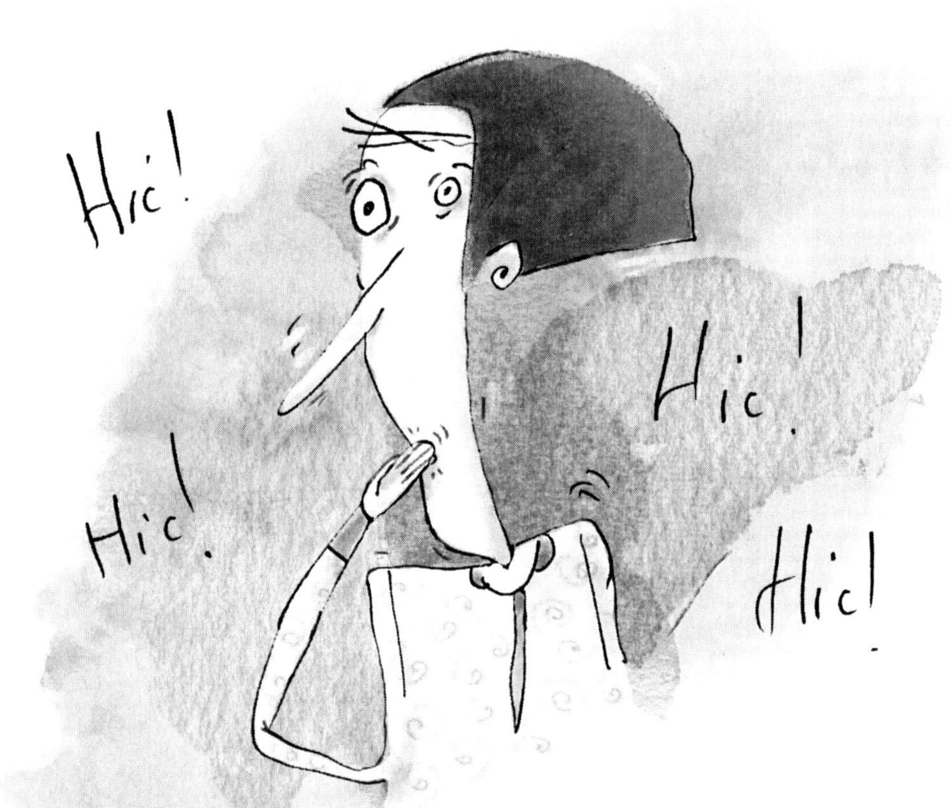
Hic!
Hic!
Hic!
Hic!

What Happened to Abigail?

No one could be prissier
Than Abigail de Lissier.

But after eating grasshopper
She hiccupped and we couldn't stop her!

Change of Heart

A beetle:
A big, black
Hard back
Crooked legged
Bug.
Ugh!

A spider:
A quick running
Slow sunning
Fang dangling
Thug.
Ugh!

A fly:
A plump bumming
Jazz humming
Window skimming
Lug.
Ugh!

But if they floss 'em
toss 'em
sauce 'em
And they heat 'em
Would you eat 'em?

THE BUG HOUSE Pie Contest

The Bug House has a contest
Aunt Nellie wants to try.
The rules say, "Bake a zingy
Extra-ordinary pie!"

She wonders about lightning bugs,
Or maybe earwig eyes.
What filling would you recommend
To help her win the prize?

Snake Waiters I

At *The Bug House*
You will find
Our waiters have a tendency
To w
      i
         n d.
But relax—
They do not bite,
Though they may **SQueeZE**
A little tight.

Snake Waiters II

Oops, I didn't mean to splat
Bug Soda on your winter hat.

What is wrong I cannot tell,
But I am feeling quite unwell.

Oh My Goodness! Look at me!
I am splitting, can't you see?

There, I'm done! Now this is dandy,
My old skin will come in handy.

Just a moment, while I stoop
And add a little to your soup.

The Delivery Bat

Good thing I can see at night
when I'm asked to make a flight.

I can get there in a flash,
leave the dinner, get the cash.

This next order's full of lice,
soaked in nectar, sopped with spice.

'Though I know it isn't right—
do you think they'd miss a bite?

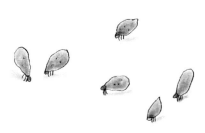

Millipede of the New Millenium

It bathes inside a big, glass tub,
And every day
It grows.
Reporters ask how big it is
But truly,
No one
Knows.

I wonder what they feed it,
But that's a secret too.
Once I saw a ketchup bottle,
Maybe that's a clue.

I've heard them say in whispers
It will feed a group of eight.
I've lots of questions for the cook . . .
I wonder why he's late . . .

Bug in Hiding

I've a pet tarantula
I love him like a brother
(And prob'ly more, although it's not
a thing I'd tell my mother.)

I've seen *The Bug House* posters
And I'm growing quite afraid.
I've double locked my spider's cage
Preparing for a raid.

I've shut the windows, barred the doors,
Oh! I expect the worst.
But if they come to get him, well,
They'll have to take me, first!

The Inspection

The Health Board came one Monday
To scrutinize for germs;
They shuddered at the jugs of bugs
And cupboards full of worms.

"Clean this up!" they hollered,
"Or we'll run you out of town!"
The owner—Mrs. Sparrow—
Pleaded, "Wait, don't close us down!"

"You'll find," she said, "Our insects
are as clean as they can be."
She bent and squeaked a feeler
In the Insect Ratatouille.

The Health Board stayed for coffee
And they ended up impressed—
"This Royal Jelly's tasty,
and your Bee Buns are the best!"

The Prayer of the Praying Mantis

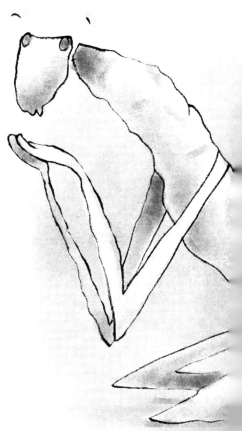

Let me not be
Called a sinner,
Let my thorax
Not grow thinner
Let me shine
And glow and glimmer
And please let me
Not be
Dinner.

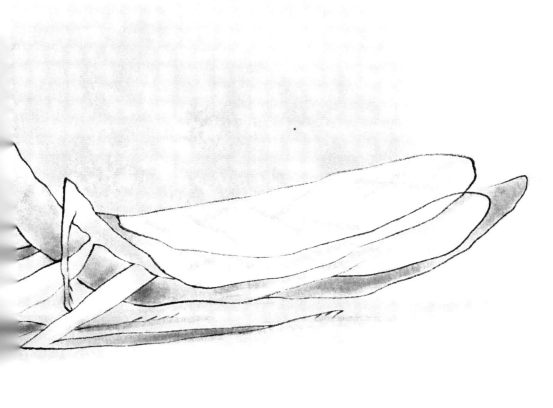

Burgers for Six

Beetleburgers, beetleburgers,
I can smell them fryin'!
Beetleburgers, beetleburgers,
That's what I'll be buyin'!

One is for my Mother,
Who likes a little cheese.
One is for my Father,
The Hungry Size, with bees.

One is for my Sister,
Who wants a whole wheat bun.
One is for my Brother,
Who asked for his well-done.

One is for our Granny—
Our family centenarian.
And so that's five in total.
For me? I'm vegetarian . . .

Dedicated to my brother Jack who swallowed a grasshopper while driving our mother along a prairie road.

A Forced Feeding

My brother wasn't keen to eat
Anything with wings or feet.

Then one day when he was driving
Windows down, a storm arriving,

Music blaring, mouth wide open
In flew..something! He was chokin'!

Didn't have a chance, that 'hopper
What you'd call a belly flopper!

Now a customer each night
Jack just loves his food in flight.

The Owner's Story

People often ask me
How my business got its start.
And truthfully, I tell them
That my sister played a part.

Maria loved the crawlies,
So I dreamed up lots of dishes.
And then one day I sampled one
And cried out, "How delicious!"

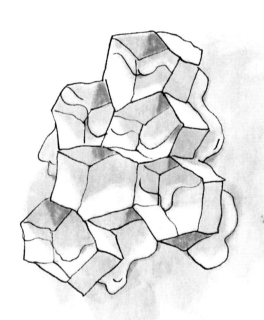

Afterword

For the flutter in your gut
And the tremor in your belly
There is nothing quite so settling
As a taste of Royal Jelly.

Acknowledgements

Thank you to the grade 3/4 class at École Tantallon Elementary School for their positive feedback!